Contents

What is a sculpture?

A sculpture is a work of art that you can see all the way around. A person who makes a sculpture is called a sculptor.

All around
You can see this sculpture from the front, back and sides, and even from the top.

What is a
Sculpture?

Anne Civardi

FRANKLIN WATTS
LONDON•SYDNEY

First published in 2005 by Franklin Watts
96 Leonard Street, London EC2A 4XD

Franklin Watts Australia
45-51 Huntley Street, Alexandria, NSW 2015

© Franklin Watts 2005

Editor: Caryn Jenner
Design: Sphere Design
Art director: Jonathan Hair
Picture research: Diana Morris

The publisher wishes to thank Fiona Cole for her assistance in making this book.

Acknowledgements:
Arte & Immagini Srl/Corbis: 10. Peter Beck/Corbis: 18. Trustees of the British Museum: 8cr.
© Barry Flanagan, courtesy Waddington Galleries. Exhibited at the New Centre Sculpture Park &
Gallery, Roche Park: 8cl. Kevin Fleming/Corbis: front cover cl, 19r. Government Art Collection ©
Andy Goldsworthy: 23 Ice Star (Scaur Water, Penpont, Dumfriesshire). Robert Harding Picture
Library © the artist: 27. Jan Isachen/Images de France/Alamy. © ADAGP, Paris & DACS,
London 2004: 15. Gail Mooney/Corbis: 9. The work illustrated on the front cover, p 17 and p 28
has been reproduced by permission of the Henry Moore Foundation. © Henry Moore Foundation.
Museum Ludwig, Cologne. © ADAGP, Paris & DACS, London 2004: front cover r: 21. Private
Collection. © ARS, New York & DACS, London 2004: 25. Private Collection/Bridgeman Art
Library: 7. Josph Sohm/Corbis: 26. Wakefield Museums & Galleries, West Yorkshire/Bridgeman
Art Library. © Bowness, Hepworth Estate: 11.

Additional photographs taken by Ray Moller.

Every attempt has been made to clear copyright. Should there be any inadvertent omission please
apply to the publisher for rectification.

A CIP catalogue record for this book is available from the British Library

ISBN 0 7496 5556 9

Printed in Hong Kong/China

Degas wanted his sculpture to look like a real ballerina. She is even wearing real clothes!

◀ *The Little Dancer Aged Fourteen*, **Edgar Degas, 1879-81** Sculptors use all sorts of materials, such as **clay**, stone or wood, to make their sculptures. This sculpture is made from a metal called **bronze**.

Where to see sculptures

You can find sculptures in
many different places, such as . . .

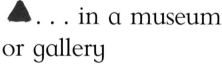 . . . in a museum
or gallery

▲ . . . in a park

Sculpture spotting
Try to spot some sculptures
when you are out and about.

▲ . . . or in a
temple or church.

Imagine! The nose of this statue is about as big as you are!

◀ **The Statue of Liberty, Auguste Bartholdi, 1884**
This famous sculpture is on an island in New York in the United States. The statue is so big that it can be seen for miles around.

How do sculptures look?

Some sculptures look like real people, animals or objects. This style is called **realistic**. Other sculptures are simple shapes and forms. This style is called **abstract**.

▶ **French statue of the Virgin and Child, 14th century**
This is a realistic sculpture. Look at the **detail** of the faces and clothes. These details make the sculpture look very lifelike.

Different styles
Both of these sculptures show a mother and a baby. Which style do you like better? Why?

▲ *Mother and Child,*
Barbara Hepworth, 1934
Look at the shapes and curves of this
abstract sculpture. Can you see the
faces, arms or legs of the two figures?

How do sculptures feel?

The way a sculpture feels is called its **texture**. A sculpture may feel hard or soft, rough or smooth.

Textured tortoise
How would this stone tortoise feel if you touched it?

Feel it
Feel some objects around your house or in your classroom. Use these words to help describe them.

rough   hard   furry   smooth   wet
dry   soft   cold   flat   bumpy   slippery

A real elephant's skin is wrinkly and rough. Does this elephant have the same texture?

Smooth skin
The sculptor used **files** and sandpaper to make this wooden elephant smooth.

Colourful sculptures

Sometimes sculptors use different colours to paint their sculptures.

Colour change
Use modelling clay to make three sculptures that look the same. See how they change when you paint them different colours and patterns.

🔺 **Painted mask**
Look at the dark colours of this mask. Do the colours make it look scary or funny to you? Notice the big red eyes and mouth.

Look at the water squirting from this sculpture's head.

▲ *Firebird*, Niki de Saint Phalle, 1983
This colourful sculpture is part of a big fountain. How many colours can you see? How do the colours make you feel?

Modelling

Sometimes sculptors shape soft materials, such as clay or plaster, to make sculptures. This is called **modelling**.

◀ **Shaping clay**
Sculptors shape the clay with their hands or with special tools. Sometimes the sculpture is baked in a hot oven, called a kiln, to make it hard.

Modelling magic
Use modelling clay to make your own sculpture. Think about how it will look from the front, back, sides, and from above.

How has the sculptor made the eyes of this king and queen?

▲ *King and Queen*, Henry Moore, 1952-53

This sculpture is made of bronze. Moore made a small plaster model of it first, called a **maquette**. The maquette gave him an idea of what the big finished sculpture would look like.

Carving

Some sculptures are made by carving away material, such as stone or wood.

◀ **How to carve**
This sculptor is using a **mallet** and **chisel** to chip away at a big block of stone. When she taps the mallet, the sharp chisel cuts off bits of stone.

How was it made?
When you see a sculpture, look at it carefully. Try to guess what material it is made from and how it was made.

► **Native American totem pole**
This totem pole was carved from the trunk of a tall tree and then painted. Each face on the totem pole is different.

◄ **Dancing bear**
A sculptor carved this bear from stone. Then he polished it to make it smooth and shiny.

Building sculptures

Sometimes sculptors put objects together to make a sculpture. This is called **constructing**.

▲ Found objects

These colourful sculptures are made from objects the African sculptor found, such as old tin cans, scraps of wire and plastic telephone cable.

Recycled robot

Look around for things that you can use to make a sculpture. Can you guess what was used to make this robot?

▲ *Balouba III*, Jean Tinguely, 1961
What objects has Tinguely used to
make this sculpture? There is even a
motor that makes the sculpture move.

Natural sculptures

Sculptors also use things they find in nature to make sculptures.

◀ The natural look

This sculptor used feathers and old animal bones to make her sculpture. The different objects have different textures.

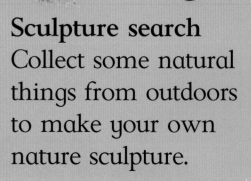

Sculpture search

Collect some natural things from outdoors to make your own nature sculpture.

▲ *Ice star,* Andy Goldsworthy, 1987
This sculpture is made of ice.
What do you think happened to it
when the sun shone on it?

Sculptures that move

The sculptures on these pages are hanging sculptures, called mobiles. The wind makes them move.

◀ Wood turner

This sculpture is made from lots of thin slats of wood that twist and curve. When the mobile spins quickly, the colours seem to blend together.

Mobile magic
Use coloured paper, thread and a clothes hanger to make your own mobile.

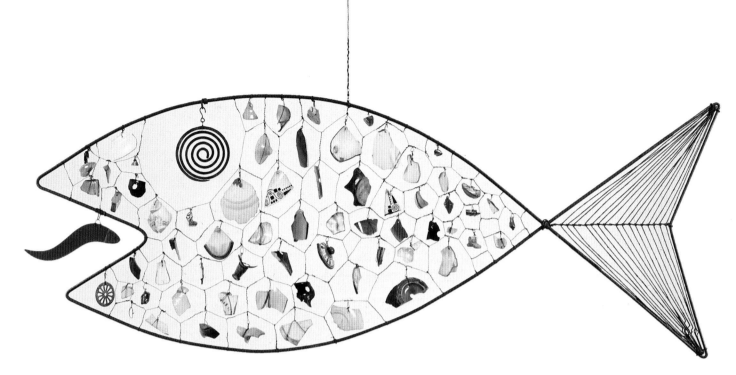

How does the sculptor make this fish look as if it has scales?

▲ *Brazilian Fish*,
Alexander Calder, 1947
Calder is famous for
making mobiles. He
made this hanging fish
from scraps of metal,
glass and pottery.

Giant sculptures

Sculptures can be any size.
Some sculptures are enormous.

▲ *Mount Rushmore,*
Gutzon Borglum,
1927-41
Four hundred workers
carved this huge
sculpture into the side
of a rocky mountain.

What's the big idea?
Imagine that you are making
a giant sculpture. What
would you make? What
material would you use?
Where would you put it?

▲ *Angel of the North*, Anthony Gormley, 1995-98
This giant angel sculpture is made of metal. It is so big that its feet are as tall as a person. The sculpture stands near a busy motorway, where lots of people see it.

Quiz

1. Is this sculpture abstract or realistic? Find more abstract and realistic sculptures in the book.

2. What texture does this sculpture have? Find more sculptures in the book with a similar texture.

3. Find sculptures in the book that are made of wood, stone or metal.

4. Look through the book to find at least 10 carved sculptures.

5. Was this sculpture modelled or constructed? Look through the book to find other sculptures that have been modelled or constructed.

Glossary

abstract A style of sculpture that is based on line and shape. Abstract sculptures do not usually look lifelike.

bronze A kind of metal that is often used for sculpture.

chisel A tool used for carving wood or stone.

clay A type of earth that is easy to model when it is mixed with water.

constructing Building a sculpture from different objects or materials.

detail The smallest, finest parts of a sculpture that make it look lifelike, such as hairs, veins or texture.

file A tool used to give stone and wood a smooth finish.

mallet A hammer used to hit the end of a chisel when carving.

maquette A small model that gives a sculptor an idea of what the finished sculpture will look like.

modelling Making a sculpture by shaping a soft material.

realistic A style of sculpture that is made to look lifelike.

texture How things feel, for example, rough or smooth.

Websites

www.sculpture.org
International website with lists of places around the world where sculptures are on display.

www.henry-moore-fdn.co.uk
Information about Henry Moore's life and work, with online galleries.

www.sculpture.org.uk
Online gallery featuring many different kinds of modern sculptures.

www.sculpturebythesea.com
Online gallery of sculptures from an annual outdoor exhibition in Australia.

Note to parents and teachers
Every effort has been made by the Publishers to ensure that these websites are suitable for children. However, because of the nature of the Internet, it is impossible to guarantee that the contents of these sites will not be altered. We strongly advise that Internet access is supervised by a responsible adult.

Index